# NATIVE AMERICAN RIVALRIES

*Susan Katz Keating*

MASON CREST
PHILADELPHIA

# NATIVE AMERICAN LIFE

# NATIVE AMERICAN RIVALRIES

*Susan Katz Keating*

SENIOR CONSULTING EDITOR DR. TROY JOHNSON
PROFESSOR OF HISTORY AND AMERICAN INDIAN STUDIES
CALIFORNIA STATE UNIVERSITY

 MASON CREST
PHILADELPHIA

To my own small tribe: Erin, Kelly, and Courtney.

Mason Crest
450 Parkway Drive, Suite D
Broomall, PA 19008
www.masoncrest.com

© 2014 by Mason Crest, an imprint of National Highlights, Inc.

Printed and bound in the United States of America.

CPSIA Compliance Information: Batch #NAR2013. For further information,
contact Mason Crest at 1-866-MCP-Book

First printing
1 3 5 7 9 8 6 4 2

Library of Congress Cataloging-in-Publication Data

Keating, Susan Katz.
  Native American rivalries / Susan Katz Keating.
     pages cm. — (Native American life)
  Includes bibliographical references and index.
  ISBN 978-1-4222-2975-0 (hc)
  ISBN 978-1-4222-8862-7 (ebook)
  1. Indians of North America—Wars—Juvenile literature.  I. Title.
  E81.K43 2013
  970.004'97—dc23
                                          2013007318

Native American Life series ISBN: 978-1-4222-2963-7

**Frontispiece: Warring tribes fight a pitched battle within sight of the walls
of Fort Mackenzie in Wyoming.**

# TABLE OF CONTENTS

# INTRODUCTION

For hundreds of years the dominant image of the Native American has been that of a stoic warrior, often wearing a full-length eagle feather headdress, riding a horse in pursuit of the buffalo, or perhaps surrounding some unfortunate wagon train filled with innocent west-bound American settlers. Unfortunately there has been little written or made available to the general public to dispel this erroneous generalization. This misrepresentation has resulted in an image of native people that has been translated into books, movies, and television programs that have done little to look deeply into the native worldview, cosmology, and daily life. Not until the 1990 movie *Dances with Wolves* were native people portrayed as having a human persona. For the first time, native people could express humor, sorrow, love, hate, peace, and warfare. For the first time native people could express themselves in words other than "ugh" or "Yes, Kemo Sabe." This series has been written to provide a more accurate and encompassing journey into the world of the Native Americans.

When studying the native world of the Americas, it is extremely important to understand that there are few "universals" that apply across tribal boundaries. With over 500 nations and 300 language groups the worlds of the Native Americans were diverse. The traditions of one group may or may not have been shared by neighboring groups. Sports, games, dance, subsistence patterns, clothing, and religion differed—greatly in some instances. And although nearly all native groups observed festivals and ceremonies necessary to insure the renewal of their worlds, these too varied greatly.

Of equal importance to the breaking down of old myopic and stereotypic images is that the authors in this series credit Native

Americans with a sense of agency. Contrary to the views held by the Europeans who came to North and South America and established the United States, Canada, Mexico, and other nations, some Native American tribes had sophisticated political and governing structures— that of the member nations of the Iroquois League, for example. Europeans at first denied that native people had religions but rather "worshiped the devil," and demanded that Native Americans abandon their religions for the Christian worldview. The readers of this series will learn that native people had well-established religions, led by both men and women, long before the European invasion began in the 16th and 17th centuries.

Gender roles also come under scrutiny in this series. European settlers in the northeastern area of the present-day United States found it appalling that native women were "treated as drudges" and forced to do the men's work in the agricultural fields. They failed to understand, as the reader will see, that among this group the women owned the fields and scheduled the harvests. Europeans also failed to understand that Iroquois men were diplomats and controlled over one million square miles of fur-trapping area. While Iroquois men sat at the governing council, Iroquois clan matrons caucused with tribal members and told the men how to vote.

These are small examples of the material contained in this important series. The reader is encouraged to use the extended bibliographies provided with each book to expand his or her area of specific interest.

Dr. Troy Johnson
Professor of History and American Indian Studies
California State University

# 1 Native American Rivalries

The fat flames crackled and shone against the dark night sky. All around the outer edges of the bonfire, a group of Cherokee warriors danced the *A te yo hi*, which means "going around in a circle." The men had been dancing this special war dance all night. Soon, they would go into combat against a fierce rival—not white settlers, but another Native American tribe living in what is now the southeastern United States.

The Cherokees were not the only native tribe to fight other natives. Long before Europeans arrived in the Americas, tribes maintained bitter rivalries and from time to time shed one another's blood. In this they were no different from the powerful European nations, such as Spain, France, and England. These nations, too, constantly struggled to be richer and more powerful than their rivals. And, when they thought it would serve their interests, they were not afraid to go to war in pursuit of those goals.

Their faces covered with war paint, modern-day members of the Sioux and Cheyenne tribes reenact a battle fought by their ancestors. Rivalries between Native American tribes frequently led to bloodshed.

Just as with the various European nations, Native American warfare took different forms and was fought for different reasons. It is also important to note that, just as the European countries were each separate, independent, **sovereign** nations, so were the Native American tribes. They had traditional friends with whom they traded and traditional enemies with whom they fought.

In California, the tribes were mostly peaceful and friendly. When they did fight, the conflict was usually confined to small groups within a family or village. Fighting was done mostly in **retaliation** for witchcraft or violence or over the right to hunt or fish in certain areas.

In the East and in Central and South America, warfare was part of tribal culture and was well organized. Large, powerful tribes waged all-out war over land rights and trade agreements. They formed **confederacies**. They conquered one another. They built empires.

Elsewhere, tribes became rivals over property. They raided herds of sheep or cattle. They stole one another's horses, which were highly prized. They kidnapped women and children and used them as slaves. Tribes formed **alliances**. They burned enemy villages and destroyed crops.

Many of the disputes have long faded from memory or are told in a mixture of truth and myth, so that no one knows exactly why or how certain tribes first became rivals. Other rivalries persisted through the years. At least one old rivalry in the Southwest has left a **legacy** that is felt even to this day.

As with rivalries between modern nations, Native American

rivalries often simmered with tension without actually erupting into warfare. When the tribes did declare war, they proceeded with great solemnity.

In addition, the tribes had special rituals before war. The Cherokees, for instance, danced the *A te yo hi.* Other tribes routinely consulted the spirits for advice before a battle and prayed for protection. They believed that magical and mystical things could happen in warfare: a

An Iroquois warrior scalps a defeated enemy in this 18th-century print.

warrior could turn himself into a bird, or rocks could become men. Ghosts of fallen warriors could come back to help their tribes—or take revenge on people who had betrayed them.

The tribes had different methods of fighting. Some preferred to fight in the open, whooping and yelling to frighten the enemy. Others moved silently among protective trees or along rivers in order to surprise an unsuspecting target.

After a battle, tribes honored their warriors for bravery. Many tribes gave their warriors new names based on daring acts committed

Plains Indians carried out frequent raids on rival
tribes. Shown here: Sioux and Cheyenne braves.

on the battlefield. Tribes held special ceremonies after combat. Some warriors had to purify, or cleanse, themselves after fighting the enemy. Another common practice was for returned warriors to give enemy scalps to the families of slain braves.

Surprisingly, perhaps, Native American rivalries grew even stronger after the Europeans arrived. The tribes competed with one another over who would trade with the French, British, Dutch, or Spanish newcomers. Wars erupted over who would supply the Europeans with furs. Wars intensified when native warriors replaced their traditional bows and arrows with European guns.

Just as the Native Americans formed and broke alliances among themselves, they alternately joined forces with and broke from the Europeans. The natives and the newcomers sometimes fought each other and sometimes joined one another's wars. In Canada, for example, French explorers sided with the Hurons against the Mohawks in a dispute over trading rights. In the War of 1812, between the British and the Americans, Native Americans from different tribes fought on each side of the conflict.

In the end, the Europeans became ultimate rivals of all Native American tribes. In time, all tribes were subdued and absorbed into the dominant nation. Long before that happened, however, there existed fierce rivalries between the Native Americans themselves. ⑤

13

Hiawatha, to the right in this illustration, mourns the strange death of his daughter. According to legend, the Mohawk chief afterward joined forces with a holy man and organized the Iroquois League. The league's purpose was to end the constant fighting among the neighboring Mohawk, Seneca, Oneida, Cayuga, and Onondaga tribes.

# 2 The Northeast

The Mohawk princess stood alongside her father, Chief Hiawatha. Father and daughter watched as a group of Mohawk tribesmen played a spirited game of lacrosse. As the princess walked toward a spring to get water, she called for her tribe to come look at an unusual bird. As the tribe came running, the princess was knocked down and trampled to death. She was the last of Hiawatha's three daughters to die a strange death. According to legend, a mystical peacemaker who had come to stop the fighting among tribes living around what is now the Northeastern United States had foretold all three deaths.

No one is quite sure when the events of the legend took place. But this particular legend—part truth, part magical story—talks about matters that happened around 1570. At the time, a number of tribes lived in the New York area, including the Seneca, the Oneida, the Cayuga, the Mohawk, and the Onondaga.

The five tribes fought constantly. They had blood feuds, in which they attacked other natives simply for belonging to an enemy tribe. They killed one another for revenge and waged all-out war. They fought so much that they were in danger of completely destroying themselves. According to the legend, the fighting would

A modern Native American woman holds a peace pipe. Rival tribes of the past sometimes made peace with each other in order to unite against a more powerful common enemy.

stop only as a result of something terrible: the death of the Mohawk princess.

After the princess was trampled to death by her own tribe, Chief Hiawatha was overcome with sorrow. He remembered the words of Deganawidah, a mystical holy man. Deganawidah had told the tribes that they must not fight among themselves. He also had warned that an evil spirit, one who did not want peace, would bring harm to Hiawatha.

Now that Deganawidah's warning had come true, Hiawatha left his tribe and joined the holy man. Together, the two men went from tribe to tribe, begging them to stop fighting.

Most of the chiefs agreed to stop the wars. However, one stubborn leader, the Onondaga chief Tadadaho, did not want peace. According to the legend, Hiawatha found that Tadadaho was actually the evil spirit described earlier by Deganawidah.

The legend also says that Tadadaho had snakes in his hair. Hiawatha combed out the snakes; then Tadadaho became friendly. Now the five tribes—the Seneca, the Oneida, the Cayuga, the Mohawk, and the Onondaga—joined together in one large group.

Again, no one is entirely certain how the story of Tadadaho got started. No one believes that he really had snakes in his hair. However, we do know that after Hiawatha talked to the Onondaga chief, the five tribes joined together. They called themselves the Iroquois League and promised to stop fighting one another. This did not mean they would not have disputes, but they agreed to settle arguments among themselves by communicating. They would not go to war. At long last, the tribes were at peace.

However, the peace only went so far. The Iroquois had pledged only that they would not fight each other. Their pact said nothing about making peace with other tribes who did not belong to their league. Thus, the five former enemies went back to war—this time, as a single Iroquois League combating tribes outside the league.

Now that they were united, the five were more powerful than ever

One of the many wars fought by the Iroquois League began in 1663 against the Susquehannock tribe living in the area of Pennsylvania.

The Susquehannocks were fierce warriors. They fought the Iroquois for about 12 years. For most of that time, the Susquehannocks held the upper hand against the Iroquois. However, the Susquehannocks were hit with an epidemic of smallpox. Even strong warriors fell victim to the deadly disease. The Susquehannocks lost much of their fighting force to illness.

The tribe was weakened even further when English colonial authorities in Maryland stopped supplying them with firearms. The Iroquois overpowered the Susquehannocks and sent them out of Pennsylvania and toward the Potomac River. Later, the defeated Susquehannocks were adopted into the Iroquois League. They joined the league in its wars against the Susquehannocks' old enemies, the Piscataways and the Mattawomans.

before—and also more successful. The Iroquois got rid of the Algonquian tribe by driving them completely out of the Adirondack Mountains and the upper St. Lawrence River. They fought the Mahican Confederacy, the Pocumtuc, the Montagnais, and more. In fact, the Iroquois League was so aggressive that few tribes living within striking distance were left untouched. The presence of Europeans only made the rivalries worse.

In 1535, the French sea captain Jacques Cartier settled on land just north of the St. Lawrence River in what is now Canada and claimed the land for France. More French settlers came. The French wanted animal skins and furs. The French and the local tribes began to trade with one another.

The tribes soon began to compete over who would trade with the French. The Huron, the Montagnais, and the Algonquian together rivaled one member of the Iroquois League, the Mohawk tribe.

In 1609, the French explorer Samuel de Champlain joined the fray. Aided by Champlain and his guns, the Huron group attacked a Mohawk war party and killed several Mohawk war chiefs. Later, Champlain helped attack a Mohawk stronghold. By 1610, the Huron/Algonquian/Montagnais alliance, empowered with French guns, drove out the Mohawks. The French later helped the Huron fight the Onondaga.

The Iroquois were, of course, not happy to see members of the Iroquois League suffer defeat. But the Iroquois could not strike back from a position of strength. They did not have guns. The only way to obtain guns was through trade with the French; however, the French were already allied with the Iroquois' enemies. In 1610, the Iroquois began to do business with newly arrived Dutch traders. Now the Iroquois, too, had firearms.

There ensued a remarkable tangle of alliances and **enmities**. The Iroquois fought the Huron. They took sides with the British against the French. They helped European colonists defeat other tribes. In one complex series of events, the Iroquois wound up allied with the Dutch against the colony of Maryland. Later, the government in Maryland

19

abandoned its own tribal allies, the Susquehannock, and signed a treaty with one tribe of the Iroquois League. This constant shifting of enemies and allies went on for years.

Certain weaker tribes moved to new territory in order to escape the constant threat of war. Others avoided certain rivers or routes controlled by the Iroquois. Around 1715, a sixth tribe, the Tuscarora,

**In the early 17th century the French explorer Samuel de Champlain (shown here) aided the Hurons in a fight against their Mohawk enemies. As they competed for control of North America's rich resources, the European colonial powers, especially France and Great Britain, formed alliances with Native American tribes.**

When the Iroquois and the Huron were at war, one nearby tribe worked hard to avoid being pulled into the conflict. That was the Neutral tribe, whose name means "someone who does not take sides."

joined the Iroquois Confederacy, and the group changed its name to the League of Six Nations.

By 1720, the league was the most powerful native group in North America. It controlled almost all other tribes who lived between the Atlantic Ocean and the Mississippi River and from the St. Lawrence River in Canada to the Tennessee River.

The Iroquois had different methods of dealing with a defeated enemy. Sometimes, they were content just to break up a rival league. Other times, the Iroquois adopted entire defeated tribes. At their worst, the Iroquois tortured and then killed captured warriors. They were particularly harsh in their treatment of the Huron. It was a strange **irony**: Deganawidah, the holy man whose pleas for peace first prompted the formation of the Iroquois League, was himself a Huron.

21

NATIVE AMERICAN LIFE

The Jivaro tribe of South America fought their rivals and hunted with blowguns, which fired small darts. The darts were tipped with curare, a poison that causes almost instant paralysis.

# 3 Central and South America

Yupanqui, a young Inca, was getting desperate. His tribe had been living in Cuzco, in the high mountains of Peru, for more than 200 years. But now, in 1438, Yupanqui's homeland was in great danger. The powerful Chancas from the north were preparing to invade. Yupanqui knew that the Inca territory would be lost unless his people defended themselves.

Yupanqui's own father, the Inca ruler, had already fled Cuzco. The chief was afraid that the Chancas would kill his son Urcon, the heir to the throne. Thus, the cautious chief had taken Urcon to safety at a faraway stronghold.

Alone in his homeland, Yupanqui was determined to save Cuzco. He persuaded two other tribes, the Canas and the Canchis, to help fight off the enemy.

When the Chancas attacked, they fought hard; they very much wanted to add the Inca territory to their own expanding empire. At first, the battle went in the attackers' favor. Yupanqui was horrified to see that his own forces were being overpowered.

Just when it seemed that all was lost, Yupanqui began shouting excitedly. According to legend, the stones on the battlefield began to rise and turned into soldiers. The legend says that the stone soldiers joined Yupanqui's army and helped fight the Chancas. Magic or no magic, Yupanqui's forces did indeed gain ground, and the battle changed course. The Incas repelled the invading Chancas, and Cuzco was saved.

People in Peru still talk about Yupanqui's courageous stand against the Chancas and about his amazing victory. However, the long-ago battle, retold as myth mixed with truth, was only one in a long history of fights among native rivals in Peru.

No one can be entirely sure just how far back that history reaches. The indigenous people of Peru left no written records of their exploits. However, scientists have unearthed evidence of warlike societies living in the Andes more than 1,000 years ago.

The first known military culture in Peru was the Wari Empire. The Waris conquered other tribes and spread their **influence** throughout Peru. They were harsh rulers who tried to impose their own culture on conquered tribes. Their empire finally died out around the year 1100.

This engraving depicts the first five Incan rulers. Manco Capac, the legendary founder of the Incas, is at the top.

A number of other tribes, such as the Lupacas and the Collas, developed their own chiefdoms. The various tribes fought one another often.

In 1200, according to legend, a mystical couple—Manco Capac and his sister, Mama Ocllo—founded the Incas, who called themselves "the Children of the Sun."

At first, the Incas had little power. They protected themselves against outsiders only by forming alliances with other tribes. However, things changed for the Incas after Yupanqui drove off the Chancas.

Yupanqui took over from his father and brother and took control of Cuzco. He changed his name to Pachacuti, which means "destroyer." He himself became a conqueror. For 25 years, he roamed the Andes, capturing territory from other peoples. He turned the Inca nation into a powerful and formidable empire.

Pachacuti did much to improve Cuzco. He built beautiful buildings and designed channels to bring water into the city. He sent his son, Topa, to continue the military conquests. When Pachacuti died, Topa became head of the Incas. Topa went on to expand the empire to nearly twice its size.

Eventually, the Incas controlled huge areas of land. Their territory stretched for 2,500 miles on the western coast of South America. The empire included portions of what are now Argentina, Bolivia, Chile, Colombia, Ecuador, and Peru. Some six million people were under the Incas' control.

The Incas subdued other tribes by making deals with their leaders.

The Incas did not have modern methods of communication. They did not even have a written language. Still, they needed to maintain control of an empire that spanned vast areas of rugged terrain. How, then, did the Incas manage to govern the various tribes they had conquered?

One way was to let the tribes partially govern themselves. When the Incas conquered a territory, they allowed the existing rulers to remain in place—as long as those rulers cooperated with Incan authority.

Another method of control was to impose strict rules on the people. All subjects were required to contribute a tax, in the form of labor, to the empire. In addition, ordinary citizens could not travel freely throughout the empire. They had to stay within certain areas. In this way, members of the various conquered tribes had limited contact with people from other conquered tribes. Without face-to-face communication, they had little chance of organizing a successful rebellion.

**27**

They offered to include the leaders in the Inca power structure in exchange for peaceful surrender. If the targeted leaders did not surrender, the Incas conquered them by force.

The Incas did not forget an enemy. They fought their old rivals, the Chancas, until the Chancas were nearly destroyed. A small band of Chancas managed to escape into the remote mountain territory of another tribe, the Chachapoyans.

The Chachapoyan territory was hard to reach. However, the Incas were skilled builders and engineers. They devised a series of rope

NATIVE AMERICAN LIFE

bridges that spanned the deep canyons and high ridges of the rugged Andes. They also knew how to build excellent roads. Around 1475, the Incas built a road into the Chachapoyan homeland, aiming to find the Chancas and conquer them. They were quite successful in this mission. While they were at it, they also conquered the Chachapoyans.

In time, the Incas conquered so many tribes and took over so much land that they had to work hard to keep all the territories under control. They had to put down rebellions that sprang up throughout the empire and had to defend a huge border.

In 1527, the Inca emperor Huayna Capac died. His two sons fought over who would be the new ruler. Incas chose sides, and soon the entire empire was swept into a **civil war**. Within five years another enemy would add to the disruption: **smallpox**, a deadly disease carried by Spanish conquistadors, or conquerors.

In 1532, the Spaniard Francisco Pizarro arrived in northern Peru. The Incas did not challenge Pizarro's relatively small force, however, because their civil war was still raging.

Pizarro slaughtered thousands of Incas in the north. Then he marched south toward Cuzco. Pizarro gained the trust of the Incas in

The Incas had a special name for their emperor. He was called the Sapa Inca. The position was passed down from father to son. If a Sapa Inca had more than one son, the position was not automatically handed to the oldest boy; the Sapa Inca would choose which of his sons would be his heir.

The Spanish conquistador Francisco Pizarro exploited a civil war and a smallpox epidemic to conquer the mighty Inca Empire.

Cuzco by appearing to support their side in the ongoing civil war, but he soon took power. He executed Atahualpa, the most powerful of Huayna Capac's sons. Now he was in charge of the Incas. He appointed Manco Inca, a member of the royal family, to help run the empire.

In 1536, Manco Inca tried to get rid of Pizarro. Gathering more than 100,000 Incas, he surrounded Cuzco. A huge battle ensued, during which Manco Inca's troops fought mightily. They were, after all, defending their homeland. At first, it seemed that they would win. Once again, however, a battle in Cuzco reversed course. There are no legends about stones rising up and turning into soldiers; but the Spaniards managed to rouse themselves, winning the battle and crushing Inca resistance to their rule.

The city that was once so desperately defended by the young Yupanqui was forever lost. The conqueror was not another tribe, but an outsider who captured the entire empire. §

29

NATIVE AMERICAN LIFE

# 4 North Central and Western United States and Canada

One spring day in 1830, a young Native American named Pahukatawa left his village to hunt for beaver. Pahukatawa belonged to the Skidi band of Pawnees and was a skilled trapper. He knew exactly where to look for the beaver that swam through the nearby South Loup River in what is now Nebraska.

Pahukatawa arrived at the riverbank. He crouched low on his heels, scanning the water for signs of movement. Pahukatawa did not know it, but he was being hunted himself. And the hunters were fast closing in.

Without warning, a band of warriors appeared. In a sudden frenzy of violence, they attacked the lone trapper, killing Pahukatawa.

This was not a random murder. The attack was part of a longstanding, fierce rivalry between two strong tribes: the Sioux and the Pawnees.

Each of these tribes also fought other Native Americans in the north central and western United States. The Pawnees fought the Delaware and the Cheyenne tribes. The Sioux battled the Chippewa. The rivalries stemmed from arguments

War shield of the Great Plains. The drawing of the bear, it was hoped, would give the warrior carrying the shield the bear's power.

This buffalo-hide painting shows a battle between the Sioux and their rivals the Blackfoot.

According to legend, the Chippewa thought that some of their fiercest enemies were like serpents. The Chippewa named these enemies "Sioux," a word meaning "snake."

over hunting or fishing grounds, or over horses. All were intense; however, the enmity between the Pawnees and the Sioux was especially ferocious.

Their trouble went back a long way. In the 1700s, the Pawnees controlled the territory around the South Loup River. They had full use of their hunting grounds and did not fear attack from enemy tribes.

As the years went on, other tribes moved into the area, and the Pawnees fought with the newcomers over hunting grounds. When the Pawnees went hunting, the newcomer tribes raided the unguarded Pawnee villages. Sometimes, the newcomers burned the villages to the ground.

When the Sioux arrived in the area, the Pawnees were already enemies with all the surrounding tribes. Thus, the Pawnees had no one to help them fight the powerful Sioux. After much warfare, the Sioux drove the Pawnees from their villages. The Pawnees built new villages on higher ground that was easier to defend, and the Pawnees and the Sioux continued to fight.

Once, a Pawnee war party attacked a Sioux camp, killing a number of Sioux. They also kidnapped a group of women and children and brought

33

NATIVE AMERICAN LIFE

them back to the Pawnee village. What they didn't know was that the captives were infected with deadly smallpox. The disease quickly spread through the Pawnee village, killing about 2,000 members of the tribe.

The Pawnees and the Sioux each knew that the other was a strong enemy. They told war stories and mystical legends about each other. They also had legends about themselves.

For example, the Sioux told many tales about a tribesmen of theirs known as Red Leaf. He had blonde hair and stood more than six feet tall. Everyone knew that Red Leaf was a great warrior. The Sioux also believed that Red Leaf could see the future.

Once, when the Sioux were getting ready to fight the Pawnees, Red Leaf told his fellow warriors that they would encounter a left-handed Pawnee who had one white eye. Red Leaf warned that the man was very dangerous.

The battle began. Among the Pawnees was the very man Red Leaf had talked about—a left-handed warrior with one white eye. This man fought with incredible fury, injuring many men and killing one of the best Sioux warriors.

As the battle raged on, a group of Sioux killed the white-eyed

American artist George Catlin
painted this skirmish between
the Sioux and their Sauk and
Fox enemies in the 1840s.

The Sioux tribe did not force their warriors to fight. A man could decide to leave a war party, even while at camp on the night before a battle. However, the tribe believed he should leave only for good reason. If a man left a war party because he was sick, no one bothered him. If he left because he lost his nerve and was afraid to fight, the other warriors viewed him with *scorn*. When the frightened warrior left camp, the remaining warriors barked at him like dogs. They wanted the sound to follow him so that he knew he was held in disgrace.

warrior. They took his necklace and medicine pouch. Seven grains of corn spilled from the medicine pouch onto the ground.

Red Leaf was angry. He said it was wrong to take the pouch. He predicted that in the next battle, seven Sioux warriors would die—one for each of the seven grains of spilled corn. The next spring, Red Leaf's prediction came true. Some feared that the prediction had actually been a curse designed to punish the warriors for acting improperly.

The Pawnees also had mystical legends. One of their favorite stories was about the young trapper Pahukatawa.

After Pahukatawa was killed, strange things started happening

A warrior of the Great Plains stands outside his tepee, holding his rifle and the reins of his horse.

37

NATIVE AMERICAN LIFE

**The famed Sioux leader Sitting Bull made this
drawing of himself, as a young warrior, riding
down a brave from a rival Plains tribe.**

among the Skidis. The tribe did well in battle against the Sioux. Skidi
warriors talked of being helped by a magical white wolf. They were
certain that the wolf was really the spirit of Pahukatawa.

The boy's spirit supposedly visited Pahukatawa's family. It also
appeared to the Skidi chief, Big Ax, and warned him about an attack
by the Sioux.

The Skidis were thrilled to hear this news, but their luck soon
changed. Things started going badly for them in battles against the
Sioux. The Skidis believed that both their chief and Pahukatawa's

brother had been rude to the boy's spirit and that now Pahukatawa was angry. The Skidis thought that their former tribesman was now helping the enemy. The Skidis blamed Pahukatawa for their troubles.

However, the tribes caused one another plenty of trouble without the help of supernatural beings. During the U.S. government's wars against the Native Americans, Pawnee tribesmen helped the United States cavalry wage war against the Sioux. In 1873, a public marksmanship competition nearly turned into all-out war between the Pawnees and the Sioux. The following year, the Sioux killed 350 Pawnees in a surprise attack.

Even as it became increasingly clear that white Americans would overpower all the Native American nations, the Sioux and the Pawnees continued to fight. The one thing they agreed on was that they were enemies. 

39

# 5 The Southwest and West

In 1996, the Navajo (these people actually refer to themselves as the Dené) world buzzed with great excitement. Something strange was going on in the remote town of Rocky Ridge, Arizona. Sarah Begay, a 61-year-old Navajo woman, said that two mysterious older men had visited her and her mother. The men warned Sarah that if the Navajos lost their traditional ways, the entire tribe would be in danger. Then, the men vanished.

Sarah's story quickly spread. The Navajos said that the visitors were deities, or gods. The tribe decided to build a **shrine** at Rocky Ridge. Sarah was worried. She thought that if a shrine were built, members of the Hopi tribe would tear it down. Sarah's house was on land the Hopis said belonged to them. The Navajos and Hopis were embroiled in

Kit Carson, an army scout and Indian agent, played a large part in defeating the Navajos in 1863. Though his tactics were often ruthless—he tried to starve the Navajos by destroying their livestock and crops, for example—Native Americans generally respected him as an honest and honorable man.

an angry land dispute that most people say dates back to 1868. However, problems with these two tribes and others in the area can be traced back for hundreds and hundreds of years.

The Navajos and Hopis live in an area of the Southwest where four states—Arizona, New Mexico, Utah, and Colorado—meet. This area is known as the Four Corners. In the late 13th century, many tribes lived here.

A great **drought** began in 1276. For more than 20 years, there was little rain. Plants did not grow. Animals died from lack of food and water. The people who lived in the Four Corners area grew hungry.

They had to work harder and harder just to feed themselves.

Navajo hunters started to range farther and farther from home in their search for **game**. They searched on land that belonged to other tribes. Over time, neighboring tribes grew angry. They accused the Navajos of **poaching**, or hunting on land that was not theirs. Some of the tribes merely complained about Navajo hunting practices.

The sun sets over the southwestern desert. The Navajo and Hopi tribes began fighting over their lands in the Four Corners area around 1868.

In early Comanche society, a chief earned his position by showing great skill and bravery in war. Once he became chief, however, he often spoke against war and advised his tribe to resolve disputes with other tribes through peaceful means.

However, one group, the Ute tribe, was particularly angry. The Utes wanted to retaliate, or strike back, against the Navajos. They staged a number of surprise attacks on Navajo farms, inflicting much damage. These attacks continued for years.

The tribes of the Four Corners continued to battle one another over hunting and land rights for hundreds of years. They shifted alliances, or friendships, back and forth. In the 1770s, the Utes and Navajos joined together against the Hopis. In 1789, the Utes switched sides and helped the Spanish fight the Navajos and the Comanches. The Utes continued to fight the Navajos into the 1800s.

In the mid-1800s, something happened that would eventually lead to the problems that continue to this day between the Navajos and the Hopis.

For many years, the Navajos and the Apaches had been raiding white settlements in New Mexico, stealing thousands of sheep, cattle, and horses. The Navajos even took cattle belonging to a United States Army general, Stephen Kearny. The general was furious and tried to stop the raids.

During the Civil War, when the Americans were busy fighting each other, the Native Americans plagued the settlers even more. In 1863, Colonel Kit Carson was sent to stop the Navajo raids. He and his men destroyed the Navajos' livestock and crops and chased tribal members into remote areas. Many people were killed.

In 1864, the Navajos surrendered and were sent to Bosque Redondo at Fort Sumner in eastern New Mexico. The Navajos had to walk 300 miles to get to the camp. Everyone went, even women and children. Many Navajos died while on the difficult journey. The strong ones survived what the Navajos now call the Long Walk. In all, about 8,500 members of the tribe were held captive at Fort Sumner. Those who survived the Long Walk had to endure horrible living conditions, polluted water, and disease.

The Navajos were forced to stay in the camp for four years. When they got out, however, they could not go back to their old lives. The U.S. government had divided the land into **reservations**. Their homes and

Navajo raiders enraged General Stephen W. Kearny by stealing his cattle.

45

Warriors in Florida attack a rival's village with flaming arrows in this 16th-century illustration. Although tribal warfare always existed, the arrival of Europeans in the New World may have made it worse.

 **The Southeast**

It was March 27, 1814. Thousands of Creek warriors were fighting against U.S. Army troops at a horseshoe-shaped section of river in east-central Alabama. Major General Andrew Jackson, who would later become president of the United States, led the Americans. At the time, Jackson was fully engaged in the army's war against the Creeks. This particular battle was called the Battle of Horseshoe Bend.

This was a bloody, violent battle. Cannon shells exploded all around, and the air was thick with the smoke of many fires. American soldiers and native warriors struggled to kill each other and to escape death themselves. As the fighting became even more intense, a Cherokee chief named Junaluska saw that General Jackson's life was in danger. A Creek warrior was about to stab Jackson with a bayonet. Junaluska rushed forward, killing the Creek warrior and saving the American general's life.

Jackson went on to lead his troops to victory in the Battle of Horseshoe Bend. The battle turned out to be the turning point in the Americans' war against the Creeks. Some people believe that the Cherokee warrior Junaluska made the American victory possible.

Junaluska's act may seem odd. Why would an native save an

American general who was fighting other native warriors? However, Junaluska's deed was not at all unusual.

For centuries, the Cherokees had fought against the Creeks. The enmity between the two tribes was so strong that Cherokee warriors were happy to join others who would help fight their rivals. However, the Creeks were not the Cherokees' only enemy. The Cherokees had many longstanding rivalries with other tribes living in what is now the southeastern United States.

In the 17th century, the Cherokees had problems with neighboring Creeks, Chickasaws, Catawbas, and Choctaws. These enemies lived in the area surrounding Cherokee lands. The Cherokees were nearly always at war with one or another of these tribes.

One of the greatest warriors of all time was a Choctaw chief named Pushmataha. Born around 1764 in what is now Mississippi, Pushmataha did not like to talk about his parents. If asked about his background, he would say, "I am a Choctaw." Once, he said, "Pushmataha has no ancestors; the sun was his father; the moon, his mother."

In truth, natives from another tribe had killed Pushmataha's parents. The killers may have been from the Creek tribe. This would help to explain why Pushmataha hated the Creeks. In 1813, Pushmataha and 700 of his warriors helped the American general Andrew Jackson defeat the Creeks at the Battle of Horseshoe Bend.

Native American warriors of the Southeast with long bows and arrows. After the introduction of the horse, bows got smaller because warriors needed to be able to maneuver their mounts.

Combat was so much a part of Cherokee life that the tribe developed a highly organized system for waging war. There were certain methods for responding to an attack, for starting a revenge war, and for dealing with other types of fights.

Many Native American tribes performed a version of the "scalp dance" to celebrate battle victories. The scalps of slain enemies— sometimes even women and children—were displayed as trophies.

The Cherokees had a special group devoted to waging war. That group was called the Red Organization. The leader was the High Priest of War, also called "the Raven." In time of war, the Raven went ahead of the war party and spied on the enemy.

Other members of the Red Organization included a healer to treat the wounded, **scouts** to help gather information, a priest who carried the sacred fire, and a special unit of women who decided what to do with prisoners of war. Messengers and flag-bearers also belonged to the group.

Before going into battle, Cherokee warriors practiced certain rituals. Sometimes they chewed on a special root and spat out the juice on their bodies. They believed that the juice would protect them against enemy weapons. They bathed at certain times and in certain ways. They prayed and they **fasted**.

The Cherokees liked to consult the spirit world to learn the course of a coming battle. They looked for signs in the way a fire burned or in the way a bead moved in the war priest's hand. The Cherokees also believed that their war priest, the Raven, could go forward a distance of two days' march to spy on the enemy and then be back in camp the next morning.

The Raven had a magical crystal that was used to predict the future. The Cherokees believed that the Raven could send his crystal into the enemy's camp. If the crystal returned covered with blood, the Cherokees felt sure they would win the coming fight.

During a battle, the High Priest of War could never retreat. If he was in danger, or if the Cherokees were losing, other warriors grabbed him and pulled him from the battlefield.

**53**

Cherokee warriors painted their war clubs red because that was considered the color of success. The color of failure was blue. Part of a prayer for warriors included the words, "Instantly grant that they shall never become blue."

After the war party returned home, the members could not go back to their families for 24 days. First, they had to be purified. At the end of the 24 days, the tribe consulted a magical crystal to learn how long they would remain at peace.

In 1660, the Cherokees came up with a way that they thought would help to ensure longer periods of peace. Large numbers of Shawnees were moving into the area. The Shawnees were running from their own enemies, the Iroquois. The Cherokees thought that the friendly Shawnees could serve as a buffer, or barrier, between the Cherokees and their surrounding enemies. The Cherokees allowed the Shawnees to settle in parts of South Carolina, between the Cherokees and the Catawbas, and in Tennessee, as a buffer against the Chickasaws.

However, the solution backfired. The Shawnees were not entirely peaceful. In 1692, when the warriors from a major Cherokee village were gone on a winter hunt, Shawnees raided the village for slaves. Worse yet, the Shawnees attracted trouble. War parties of Iroquois came south to attack their old enemy. While in the area, the Iroquois also attacked the Cherokees.

When a Cherokee Great War Chief retired, he was honored at a special ceremony. At the ceremony, the tribe gave him an eagle feather. The feather was painted with one red stripe for each war party the chief had led and for each enemy he had slain in battle.

It was not the last time the Cherokees would regret making an alliance. Much later, in 1828, the U.S. government started moving Native Americans from their homelands. The government pressured the Cherokees to sign an agreement saying that they would move to Indian Territory. Among those who refused to move was Junaluska, who had saved Andrew Jackson's life during the Battle of Horseshoe Bend.

Junaluska was still a chief, and now Jackson was president of the United States. Jackson had said he would never betray the Cherokees. Junaluska went to Jackson to remind him of the long-ago promise. Junaluska wanted the president to help the Cherokees, but Jackson refused. The Cherokees wound up being forcibly removed from their homeland. Afterward, Junaluska said of Jackson: "If I had known he would break his oath, I would have killed him that day at the Horse Shoe." §

# CHRONOLOGY

**1200** According to legend, Manco Capac and his sister, Mama Ocllo, become the first rulers of the Inca tribe in what is now Peru.

**1276** A great drought in the American Southwest forces Native Americans to roam outside their traditional homelands in search of food and water.

**1438** Yupanqui, a young Inca, drives off the Chancas when they attack Cuzco in Peru; Yupanqui changes his name to Pachacuti and becomes ruler of the Incas.

**1492** Christopher Columbus arrives in the New World.

**1532** Spanish conquistadors under Francisco Pizarro begin their takeover of the vast Inca Empire.

**1535** French explorer Jacques Cartier settles along the St. Lawrence River in what is now Canada; his presence heightens local Native American rivalries over control of the fur trade.

**1570** Five tribes in the American Northeast join together to form the Iroquois League, also called the Iroquois Confederacy.

**1610** The Iroquois obtain firearms from Dutch traders.

**1710** The Tuscarora are the sixth tribe to join the Iroquois League.

**1775** The Revolutionary War begins in America.

**1789** The Ute join the Spanish in a fight against the Navajo and Comanche.

**1812** Britain and the United States go to war against one another.

**1814** Cherokee warriors join forces with Major General Andrew Jackson to fight the Creeks in the Battle of Horseshoe Bend in Tennessee.

**1830s** The Cherokee are removed from their homeland by order of the U.S. government.

**1863** Kit Carson fights the Navajos.

**1864** The Navajo are sent on the Long Walk to be imprisoned at Fort Sumter, New Mexico.

**1868** Navajos are released from Fort Sumner; some Navajo settle on lands claimed by the Hopis.

**1873** A public marksmanship competition nearly turns into all-out war between the Pawnee and the Sioux.

**2013** Recent government statistics indicate there are more than 5.2 million Native Americans living in the United States and Canada.

# GLOSSARY

**alliance** a friendship, usually between two or more groups or nations.

**civil war** a war between opposing groups within a country.

**confederacy** an alliance between two or more nations.

**drought** a long period of extremely hot, dry weather when there is not enough rain for crops to grow.

**enmity** mutual hatred or ill will.

**fast** to go without food voluntarily for a period of time.

**game** wild animals hunted for sport or food.

**influence** to persuade or sway somebody; to have the power to affect something.

**irony** something that is the opposite of what was expected.

**legacy** something received from an ancestor.

**poach** to trespass on other peoples' rights or land for hunting or other purposes.

**reservation** an area of land set aside for certain Native American tribes to live on.

63

# PICTURE CREDITS

# CONTRIBUTORS

**Dr. Troy Johnson** is chairman of the American Indian Studies program at California State University, Long Beach, California. He is an internationally published author and is the author, co-author, or editor of twenty books, including *Wisdom Spirits: American Indian Prophets, Revitalization Movements, and Cultural Survival* (University of Nebraska Press, 2012); *The Indians of Eastern Texas and The Fredonia Revolution of 1828* (Edwin Mellen Press, 2011); and *The American Indian Red Power Movement: Alcatraz to Wounded Knee* (University of Nebraska Press, 2008). He has published numerous scholarly articles, has spoken at conferences across the United States, and is a member of the editorial board of the journals *American Indian Culture and Research and The History Teacher.* Dr. Johnson has served as president of the Society of History Education since 2001. He has won awards for his permanent exhibit at Alcatraz Island; he also was named Most Valuable Professor of the Year by California State University, Long Beach, in 1997 and again in 2006. He served as associate director and historical consultant on the award-winning PBS documentary film *Alcatraz Is Not an Island* (1999). Dr. Johnson lives in Long Beach, California.

**Susan Katz Keating**, a former newspaper reporter and editor, is a freelance writer and educator. Her work has appeared in many publications. She is the mother of three children and lives with her family in Virginia.